To C

Hope you

(but there's a dog in it too)

THE THINKING CAT

Stephen Curtis

Other works by Stephen Curtis
A Wonderful Piece of Work, a novel, 2014
The Penguin Writer's Manual, with Martin Manser, 2002
The Bloomsbury Crossword Solver's Dictionary, with Ann Stibbs, 2004
The Facts on File Guide to Style, with Martin Manser, 2006
Perfect Punctuation, Random House, 2007
Perfect Party Games, Random House, 2010

Other works by Jessica Palmer
The Art of Papercutting, Search Press, 2015
Tangle Wood: A Captivating Colouring Book with Hidden Jewels, Search Press, 2015
Tangle Bay: An Enchanting Colouring Book with Hidden Treasures, Search Press, 2016

THE THINKING CAT

STEPHEN CURTIS

with illustrations by

JESSICA PALMER

Published by Kingsway Publishing, Bath 2016

British Library C.I.P.

A CIP catalogue record for this title is available from the British Library.

Kingsway Publishing, Bath
3 Kingsway,
Bath, BA2 2NH
UK

KingswayPubBath@aol.com

ISBN-13: 9780993131240
ISBN-10: 0993131247

DEDICATIONS

For Thomas and Sue (1984)

For Tilly, Inigo, Reuben, Lewis and Saskia (2016)

And in memory of Barnsley (1996–2015), a cat of character

THE THINKING CAT

Inside my father's bowler hat
Once lived a most peculiar cat.
My father's hat, I should explain,
Though he used to wear it on the train
When going in to work each day
Was old and worn-out now and lay
Discarded on an attic shelf –
My father put it there himself.

Now, how and when and why this cat
Had made his home inside the hat
Nobody knew. The first we heard
Were faint, faint footsteps like a bird's
Backwards and forwards in the night.
My mother woke up in a fright.
'Burglars!' she thought; she then thought 'Rats!'
(Of course she wouldn't think of cats).
She nudged my father. With a snort,
Explosive as a gun's report,
He stirred and muttered 'What?' and then
At once went back to sleep again.
Fearing for all the family treasures
My mother rose to desperate measures.
'Henry!' she cried, and roughly shook him,
'Wake up! WAKE UP!' …
                              It always took him
A full ten minutes at the best
To struggle back to consciousness
And by that time, of course, the noise

Had stopped.
        Well, now, my dad employs
Strong language if he is disturbed.
'Just listen and don't say a word,'
My mother hissed. With ears acock
They heard the ticking of the clock,
The bedsprings creak, a train go by
And early birdsong from the sky.
Of goings-on within the roof
Came not a single shred of proof.
So he called her some dreadful names,
She said that she was not to blame,
Insisted that he go and see ...
(His refusal wakened me!)
And there the matter might have stood,
Had I not been especially good.

A visit from my Great-aunt Gay
Was scheduled for the sixth of May.
Now, Great-aunt Gay was generous
With things that didn't quite suit us.
Each Christmas brought a splendid gift
(I noticed how my mother sniffed
Before she said 'How lovely!'). So,
Six wooden monkeys in a row,
A set of twelve enamel frogs,
Some plaster ducks, some china dogs,
The ballerinas in six positions,
The busts of all the great musicians
Had found their way into the attic.
There they remained aloof and static –

A most peculiar cat

Except, of course, when Great-Aunt Gay
Announced that she would come and stay.

By now I'd ceased to think it strange
That Mum should wish to rearrange
The house and all its decoration
In honour of my great-relation,
And, knowing Gay's arrival near,
What should I do but volunteer
To fetch down the entire collection.
Mum sighed 'All right,' and gave direction:
I must take care, I must not drop
A single thing, nor must I stop
To rummage round for my old toys
(She'd forgotten all about the noise).
I went upstairs and got a light
And set the ladder dead upright,
Then climbed it, fiddled with the latch
And opening up the trap-door hatch
I met, to my intense surprise,
A pair of green enormous eyes.

Starting as if I'd seen an adder,
I nearly fell back down the ladder,
And would have lost my grip, I'm sure,
And tumbled ten feet to the floor,
But for one thing which held me tight –
The eyes spoke. I went stiff with fright.
I froze, I gaped, I tried to shout
But not one sound would venture out.

I met, to my intense surprise,
A pair of green enormous eyes

Quite unperturbed my unknown saviour
Said 'This is rather odd behaviour.
Pray tell me, is it your intention
To hang all day there in suspension?
It took you long enough to call,
I thought you might not come at all.
Well, now you're here, come in, be quick.'
He turned and gave his tail a flick …
Of course, the moment he did that
I realised he was a cat.

A cat?! My feeling of relief
Was tempered with stark disbelief.
A talking cat! Could such things be
In nineteen hundred and eighty-three?
I heard Mum move about downstairs.
Could I have stumbled unawares
On some new door to fairyland?
I shook my head and pinched my hand.
The loft had its familiar smell,
Aunt Gay's menagerie as well,
The monkeys, dancers, ducks and dogs
Stood motionless as stones or logs
Showing not the slightest inclination
To sudden, magic animation.
Here was this cat so suave and formal
And all the rest was just as normal!
I found the whole thing hard to swallow,
And yet what could I do but follow?
So, switching on my torch, I stepped
In after him. At once he leapt
Upon an old trunk standing there
And fixed me with a bright green stare.

'Young man', he said, 'This will not do.
If I'm to take up house with you
I cannot cope with all this gear,
I need a bit of space up here.
So this and this, and that and that
Will have to go elsewhere, that's flat.'
He waved a magisterial paw
And jumped back down upon the floor.
'A thinking cat,' he then went on,
'Needs lots of room to think upon.
Each night before I go to bed
Such brilliant thoughts flash through my head
I need to walk them to and fro
To make sure they come out just so,
And all this stuff gets in my way.'

I didn't know quite what to say.
Should I explain, apologise,
Chase him away and damn his eyes,
Or try his purpose to distinguish,
Or compliment him on his English?
While working out just what to do
I took a somewhat closer view
Of what he looked like. He was trim
(Maybe his thinking kept him slim),
Much like a normal cat, but bigger
With six-inch whiskers and a long, lean figure.

His coat was lustrous, thick and warm
And sleek and smooth and uniform,
All silver-grey like precious metal,
Or Great-aunt Gay's best pewter kettle.
And then, of course, there were those eyes

As green and round as gooseberry pies
Without the pastry. When he walked
(In fact he almost always stalked)
He held his head with conscious pride
And lordly glanced from side to side,
As if he moved in social circles
Far, far above us lesser mortals.

'Oh!' I replied at last, 'I see,'
Deciding to go cautiously.
At this the cat swung round at once,
Concluding I must be a dunce
And swept me with a withering look;
'It seems as if I quite mistook
The kind of house I chose to visit.
Pray tell me is it not or is it
The first time you have met a cat
Who's thinker, talker, acrobat?'
(He dropped at once his lordly pose
And did a headstand on his nose.)
'You haven't even brought me cream!
I ask you, sir, what does this mean?'
'Excuse me,' I replied, 'I fear
I didn't know that you were here.
But now I know...' 'You'll fetch some milk?'
His voice was smooth as smoothest silk.
'Well – er – at least I can clear out
The things that you complained about.'
'Milk first' he purred, 'good lad, I knew
That I was right to count on you.
Now run along and come back quick.'
'Er – yes,' I said and stopped to pick
Up Bach, Beethoven, Brahms and Liszt
Stepped backward, stumbled, nearly missed

My footing on the ladder, then
Came down to daylight once again.

The fact is, I was quite bemused.
A talking cat who's not amused,
A cat who orders you about –
Such things are hard to fathom out,
Especially when it's not a dream.
Ought I to ask my Mum for cream?
I went back puzzling down the stair
And found, in fact, she wasn't there,
Which saved an awkward explanation –
It was a tricky situation.

There was some milk. I got a cup
And hastened straight away back up
To find the cat sunk deep in thought,
Perhaps of melancholy sort,
Until he saw the milk was there.
That acted like a change of air.
It took him all his self-control
Not to perform a forward roll,
Instead, with conscious dignity,
He nodded gravely once to me,
Then sniffed the milk, then licked his paw
And took a turn around the floor ...
At length he deigned to stoop and sip,
Relaxing his stiff upper lip.

When he had finished by and by
He heaved a long and heartfelt sigh.
'Ah, milk!' he said, 'you cannot beat
In winter's cold or summer's heat
Good, honest milk. Remember that

And think upon a thinking cat
Who, though not easily cast down,
Has felt the force of Fortune's frown.'

He seemed to be throwing out suggestions
That he'd respond to further questions,
But is it quite polite, I wondered
To ask directly if someone's blundered,
Worked out a plan and seen it fail,
Or lost their money and gone to jail?
(This happened to my Uncle Jim –
And no-one ever mentions him.)
Perhaps his mate had left him flat
Eloping with some thoughtless cat?
This made it quite a ticklish task
Deciding what I ought to ask ...
Something at which he would not baulk ...
Like how and why he learned to talk.

'Talking? That's nothing much,' said he,
'I heard a dog talk on TV.
Cats don't indulge in idle chatter.
Thinking is quite another matter.
It places a tremendous strain
Upon the muscles of the brain,
Which is, perhaps, the reason why
Most human beings never try.
Our skill in ratiocination
Has justly made our reputation
As helpers to the seer and sage
In every land and every age.
Egyptians worshipped as divine
A distant ancestor of mine,

Egyptians worshipped as divine
A distant ancestor of mine.

Another thought with Socrates,
One later sat on Newton's knees
Assisting him with great devotion
In framing his first law of motion.
And I myself, I must confess,
Don't feel that I've accomplished less.
I am a cat of many parts,
A bachelor of feline arts,
I catalogue and categorise
Subjects that perplex the wise
And my research in catechisms,
Cataracts and cataclysms
Has brought me honorary degrees
From several universities.

I've had a brilliant career,'
And here he paused to wipe a tear,
'That is, I once had,' he went on,
'But now my hopes and dreams are gone.
Cats, unlike dogs and mice, you see,
Are subject to catastrophe.
I ran a firm, Consult-a-Cat,
And just last week it folded flat.'

He said this in a tragic tone
That would have moved a heart of stone.
Clearly my sympathy was needed
And I felt just as sad as he did,
But hearing his life's history
Had roused my curiosity.
I felt I absolutely must
Find out just why his firm went bust,
And what had brought him down our way
And how long he was going to stay.

I ran a firm, Consult-a-Cat

'Oh dear,' I said, 'that's very bad
But when you're feeling really sad
My mother says, and I don't doubt it,
It does you good to talk about it.
I know I'm only young, but still
If I can help at all, I will.'
'Yes, yes,' he said, 'you're very kind.
I must try harder not to mind.
I've known it happen to the best,
It doesn't do to get depressed.

Thinking's a hazardous profession,
Especially in a world recession,
And intellectual resources
Are just no match for market forces.
If I may give you one small tip –
Beware, young man, the micro-chip.'
'Er – yes,' I said, 'thanks, I was thinking ...'
'That's the trouble,' he interjected.
'The information's all collected
So even the stupidest commuter
Thinks he can think with a computer.
For him, of course, that's very nice.
I end up having to catch mice.'
'Oh no', I cried,' not while you're here,
I'd like to make that very clear.
You've had bad luck; you need a rest.
Why don't you stay here as my guest?'
'Well, I was merely passing through,
But could perhaps stop a week or two.
Your milkman comes round every day...?
Hmm, it may be worth my while to stay.
Yes, get me paper, pens and thumbtacks,

It's time to think of making comebacks!
I've a new idea that might go far,
A patent medicine for catarrh,
Chocolate-flavoured, water-based,
Cheap to make and nice to taste;
Commercially it can't go wrong,
Though just to help the work along
I shall need money in advance ...
You're not rich by any chance?'
'We're not,' I said, 'I'm not quite sure
But Dad makes out we're very poor.
If it'd help I'll have a look
In my post office savings book.'
He waved his paw as if to say
'That's peanuts, but thanks anyway,'
And promptly seemed to lose himself
In musings on his future wealth.
'Oh well,' I said, 'at any rate
It's cheered you up a bit, that's great.
If you need anything at all
You know you only have to call.
I've never had a pet...' At this
He jumped up, bristled, gave a hiss
And to my utter consternation
Vanished without explanation.

But then I heard my mother calling.
She had decided I was stalling
And up to mischief in the attic.
Her tone of voice was most emphatic:
Unless I reappeared that minute
I should be well and truly in it!
So that was it. He hadn't fled

I thought I saw a tufted ear
Peep up behind a chandelier

Because of anything I'd said.
I thought I saw a tufted ear
Peep up behind a chandelier,
Apologised in that direction
And gaily went to stern correction,
Expecting shortly to renew
The interrupted interview.

I will pass over what Mum said,
How I was nearly sent to bed,
How Dad got into quite a huff
At being sent to fetch Gay's stuff –
I stuck my fingers in my ears
To make quite sure I shouldn't hear
What happened if he found my cat –
He didn't, thank the Lord for that!
So all that night and all next day
Were spent awaiting Great Aunt Gay,
Whose newest offering was a clutch
Of china rabbits, plus a hutch,
And who declared she had to see
As much as possible of me.
It was no use my making plans,
Aunt Gay had time upon her hands.
Three days passed in an agony
Of mutual civility,
Of getting out my school reports
And showing off my football shorts,
Or hearing how I'd grown and how
I'd got to be a big boy now
And mustn't slip into bad habits,

Gay's newest offering was a clutch
Of baby rabbits …

But be a pet and dust the rabbits.
I sat there guilty and dejected,
Knowing the cat must feel neglected.
Worse was to come. It was made clear
I was forbidden to go near
The attic. Mum had found me standing,
Craning upwards on the landing,
Trying desperately to catch
Footstep, scuffling, purr or scratch
Or any sound as evidence
My cat was still in residence.
Nothing direct was said, but when
I tried to volunteer again
Once Gay had gone, I soon perceived
My offer was not well received.

Of course, it had occurred to me
Perhaps the proper course might be
To tell my mother all the facts –
But then I know how she reacts.
She might believe there was a cat,
The kind that sits upon the mat
(Except when lolling in your chair
And leaving it all full of hair),
The kind that sweetly licks its paws
(Except when sharpening its claws
Upon your polished furniture),
The kind that greets you with a purr
(Except when howling all night long
Its endless eerie mating song) –

She'd believe a cat as such,
Although she wouldn't like it much

Yes, she'd believe a cat as such,
Although she wouldn't like it much,
But my feline philosopher
Would never pass. All that to her
Would simply be a pack of lies
I had made up or fantasised
As cover for some naughtiness,
Because I'd made some dreadful mess
Or else because, through thick and thin,
If I had got a kitten in
I'd stick at nothing to make sure
The poor thing wasn't shown the door.
My mother knew me through and through –
It was just as well I knew her too.

But what if she believed me? What
If Dad and she were pleased and got
To know and like my thinking friend?
I knew at once where that would end.
They'd bring in all their friends to see
Their wonderful discovery:
The cat would feel betrayed and harassed
And I'd be horribly embarrassed.
And what if, bribed with double cream,
He opted for the adult team?
I shouldn't be a bit surprised,
For cats love being lionised.

He'd lap up the publicity,
Become a great celebrity

Off to London he would go
To host his own late-night cat show

And off to London he would go
To host his own late-night cat show.
Then, after many years had passed
We two might meet again at last,
I'd be a half-forgotten voice,
Someone he'd not recall by choice
(This was the last twist of the knife),
A guest on his 'This Is Your Life'.

You see now why I couldn't say
A word about him, come what may.
I plotted, schemed, I made a vow
I'd get back to the loft somehow
But had to wait a week in fact
Before I got a chance to act.
My parents wouldn't go away.
Until, at last, that Saturday
They both went out, they said, to see
A man about a new settee,
And I was left at home to watch
Tom and Jerry on the box.

By then I was in such a state,
Almost before they'd shut the gate
I'd got the ladder and a light,
Some milk, some cheese, an egg, a bite
Of meat intended for a stew
And scrambled up without ado,
Throwing the trapdoor open wide ....
There was no trace of cat inside.
I hesitated, then I coughed –
It was hot and stuffy in the loft
And nothing stirred except the dust
That in a sunbeam whirled and fussed,

A shaft of light in that bright gloom ...
A summer silence filled the room.
But then I seemed to hear a sigh
Coming from somewhere quite close by.
'Hello?' I said, and 'Is that you?'
('Puss, puss, puss' just wouldn't do).
There came the faintest rustling sound
I quickly flashed my torch around
And dangling from my father's hat
Saw the limp tail of my dear cat.
I cheered, I cried, 'Hello, it's me,
I've brought you something nice for tea.'
He gave no answer to my call
But turned his face towards the wall.
Indeed, he did look very peaky.
His silver fur seemed somehow streaky
Where his ribs were. He'd grown thin
While I'd been away from him.
'Please, cat', I said, 'please, what's the matter?
Don't be like that.' There was a patter
Of pigeon's feet upon the tiles;
With one of those fixed feline smiles
He raised his head a moment, then
Languidly laid it down again
And in a voice by grief subdued
Uttered one word, 'Ingratitude.'

'No, no', I said, 'I'm not ungrateful
But all this week I've had my plate full,
Aunt Gay was here and then my Mum
Simply refused to let me come.
I did try hard, I didn't shirk,
It's just – well, my plans didn't work.'
He shrugged his shoulders, spread his claws
And there ensued a pregnant pause.

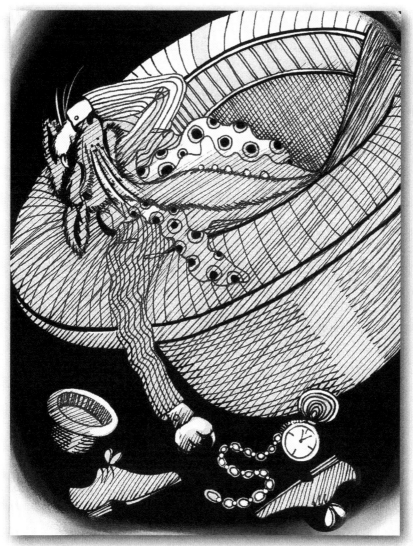

He gave no answer to my call
But turned his face towards the wall

'Here's milk,' I pleaded, 'here's some meat
And egg and cheese for you to eat.'
At last he stepped beyond the brim,
Shaking his hind legs after him,
And with a bland, indifferent stare
Inspected me and all the fare.

It would be tedious to relate
All that he did before he ate,
And how he let himself be wooed
Before he'd even touch the food
(But standing off and showing pique
Are vital to a cat's mystique).
He grew much friendlier when he'd fed.
I bent and gently stroked his head
Then ran my hand along his spine,
Feeling the fur so thick and fine,
And when he lifted up his chin
I took the hint and tickled him.
We were so familiar, so at ease
I lifted him upon my knees
And there, in spite of all his pride,
The spinning wheel in his inside,
Whirring, purring, let me know
He was content we should be so.

I do not know how long we sat
Just cat and boy and boy and cat;
It was not long enough when he,
Perhaps mindful of his dignity,

I do not know how long we sat
Just cat and boy and boy and cat

Slipped off me and began to slick
His ruffled fur with long hard licks
And, watching him, I could not wait,
I felt I had to know my fate'
I had to pop the crucial question –
Yet make it sound like a suggestion
Made casually, just off the cuff.
Could I be nonchalant enough?
'Would you perhaps,' I said, 'consider
Staying here – I mean, for ever?'
He looked up, I began to blush
And went on in a headlong rush.
'We could be friends, you'd be my cat,
You needn't live inside that hat,
I'd make you somewhere really snug
Where you could curl up on a rug.
I'd bring you milk and meat and fish,
You'd have your name upon your dish
And you'd be able to come and go
Just as you pleased. Except you'd know
Whatever place you chose to roam to
You'd always have me to come home to.'
I stopped there, for I couldn't tell
If my idea had gone down well.
Perhaps it had come out too quick –
The cat seemed frozen in mid-lick.
What was he thinking? Was he glad?
Feverishly I tried to add
Something final that might tip
The scale and seal our partnership.

'I realise you'll need time for thought,'
I said – or something of the sort.
'And if you stayed, I wonder whether
We mightn't get to think together.
They say for getting thinking done
Two heads are better than just one.'

One instant while the first shock lasted
The cat looked simply flabbergasted.
But then, as if regaining strength,
He stiffened all along his length
And, concentrating all his ire
In one long look of bright green fire,
He thundered out, 'I think alone.'
My spirits sank. I should have known,
I should have thought... He turned away.
'Come back', I said, 'I mean to say...'
'Silence!' he cried, 'I've heard enough
Of all that sentimental stuff.
Young man, I thought you had more sense.
Why, this is sheer impertinence.
Whilst I possess this expert brain
Which mesmerised the King of Spain
And brought me contacts from as far
As Muscat, Fez and Zanzibar
(From seven sheiks in point of fact)
I'll live and die a solo act.
No, do not try to be persistent,
I do not need a boy assistant.

... contacts from as far
As Muscat, Fez and Zanzibar

These paws' he said, and held them up,
'Received a jewelled loving cup
From the Sultana of Jaipore
(I may have mentioned this before)
Whose chronic cataleptic spasms
I treated with my cataplasms.
Yes, I have pawned that cup, I know,
But bear in mind, young man, that though
By various unforeseen mischances
I find myself in circumstances
Unworthy of my gifts and status,
I do not *feel* like small potatoes.
No cat who ever penned a sonnet
Eats from a bowl with "Pussy" on it!'

These proud and eloquent remarks
Spat from him like a shower of sparks.
The cat who, half an hour before,
You would have said was at death's door
Strode vigorously to and fro,
His tail erect, his eyes aglow,
Quivering with passion as he spoke.
While I could see it was no joke,
There was one slightly hopeful factor –
He did it rather like an actor.
Perhaps he had to show distaste,
Just as a way of saving face.
I'd made so many dreadful boobs,
I hadn't got a lot to lose,
And having muffed the straight approach
I thought perhaps if I could broach

The subject much more cautiously
And try a little flattery
He might be won round even yet –
This could be the only chance I'd get.

'I'm sorry, Mr. Cat', I mumbled,
Trying to sound profoundly humbled,
'I realise now I went too far,
I see more clearly how things are.
Whatever happens in the sequel
We two could never think as equals.
I just thought – well, forget all that,
Of course you wouldn't be my cat
As such, but you might find this place
Quite useful as a kind of base,
And when you'd not too much to do
I could come up and sit with you,
For listening to your conversation
Would be a first-rate education.
Please, Mr Cat…' He clicked his tongue.
'Well, you are very, very young,
And youth, of course, has ever lacked
Discretion, deference and tact.
I was a young cat once, you know,
Though that, thank God, was long ago.
Perhaps you've read the book I've written
On how to raise a problem kitten?'
I shook my head. 'Well, that can wait.
But there's one thing we must get straight.
In future interviews with me
Don't mention domesticity.'
'I won't,' I said. 'That's good,' he purred.
'The idea is of course absurd.

The life of a domestic cat
Has been described as dull, stale, flat,
Unprofitable and, in short,
Fit only for the vulgar sort.
From Persian blue to common tabby
It makes us indolent and flabby.
House cats are ignorant and untutored,
First class bores and mostly neutered.
Perhaps it's not occurred to you
The thing such cats most often do
Is sleep – on sofas, beds, and chairs
In cupboards underneath the stairs
In baskets, boxes, bistros, bars
And on the bonnets of parked cars.
Go shopping and it's no surprise
To see amidst the merchandise
A sleeping cat who, it appears,
Has gathered dust for years and years.
Don't stop to peer and wonder if
He's stuffed – more likely he's bored stiff.
On window sills outside their homes
As witless as the garden gnomes,
My lesser brethren lie and doze.
It really gets right up my nose
For humans think "How nice, how sweet,
Look how it tucks its little feet
Under its little furry chest –
Aah, is it having a lovely rest?"
Not seeing it as a sad reflection
Upon the human–cat connection.
I was not born to thoughtless slumber
So don't intend to join their number –
Not that I've not had tempting offers,

Those seven sheiks had well-filled coffers
And statesmen, film stars, V.I.Ps
Crowned heads and wealthy divorcees
Have made no secret of the fact
A thinking cat was all they lacked.
I dare not walk down Downing Street.
A certain person might entreat
My coming at the state's expense
As national cat-in-residence.
I think perhaps you might concede
You really aren't quite in that league.
In any case the principle
Is utterly invincible.
I think...'
        He thought, but what it was
I never did find out because
I heard a key turn in the lock
And realised with frightful shock
It was my father and my mother –
The cat went one way, I another.

Too late! Though I went through the hole
Just like a fireman down his pole
And scratched my hand and bruised my knee,
The great escape was not to be.
They were already in the hall
And simply stood and watched it all.

They were already in the hall
And simply stood and watched it all

I dreaded what was coming next
And tried to think up some pretext,
Something to do with Great Aunt Gay.
Not that it mattered anyway,
It was all over now, I knew,
The thinking cat and I were through.

I slunk downstairs, they simply stood.
'Is this what you call being good?'
My mother said at last, and had
A great deal more, I'm sure, to add
But Dad stepped in before the worst
And said, 'OK, but show him first.'
'I've a good mind not to,' said my Mum,
'What's happened? Have you hurt your thumb?
Well, serve you right.' She didn't budge.
My father gave her a quick nudge.
'All right', he said, 'Calm down, all right,
We'll have it out with him tonight,
But first things first. It's very hot
Let's go and get the you-know-what.'
This was a mystery to me.
Was you-know-what a new settee
Or something else?
                    Though Mum was snappy
My Dad was looking very happy.
My misdemeanours hadn't damaged
The little scene that he'd stage-managed.
'So what d'you think it is?' he said.
I looked at him and shook my head.

He flung the car door open wide
And scooped up something from inside

It was a tiny flop-eared pup

Then turned around and held it up –
It was a tiny, flop-eared pup
That wriggled, squeaked and waved its paws.
'Take him,' my father said, 'he's yours!'
'And mind you take good care of him,'
That was my mother chiming in.
'It's up to you to see he's fed
And don't let me catch him on your bed.'
I held the puppy gingerly
A little bit away from me.
It seemed to want to lick my face,
Its legs were thrashing round in space.
Dad said, 'Hey, are you sure you've got him?
Put one hand underneath his bottom.'
'You take him,' I said and rushed inside.
And that was when I broke and cried.

What happened then is not quite clear,
I know my parents thought it queer.
At first they thought their little boy
Was simply overcome with joy
Because they'd made his wish come true.
But, as there was nothing they could do
To comfort me or cheer me up –
I wouldn't even stroke the pup –
They soon found out this wasn't so.

My dad then said that he would go
And take a look around the attic.
I found this prospect so traumatic
That I began to scream and shout
And in the end it all came out.

But, though the facts were now unmuzzled,
They left my parents very puzzled.
As I foresaw, they could not tell
If I were seriously unwell,
Delirious, dreaming, or demented
Or if the story was invented,
Or if indeed there was a cat.
The only way to settle that
Was to go up aloft and see.
It took me some time to agree.
They had to reassure me twice
That they thought cats were very nice,
That any cat they found could stay,
He'd not be hurt or chased away.
So up Dad went, and soon came down
Still wearing the same puzzled frown.
'Oh no, he's gone!' I cried and dashed
Up the ladder and through the hatch,
My father following close behind.
But there was nothing left to find
Except the milk-bowl and the plate
From which before he drank and ate.
We searched each cranny, every nook,
We turned the tea-chests out and shook
The ancient curtains, sheets and cloths
Which harboured only dust and moths.
He was not there, and, which was weird,
The hat had also disappeared,
Though dad could only just recall
He'd ever kept the thing at all
And thought he'd lost it in a gale

It was as if he'd never been

Or given it to a jumble sale.
No trace, no smell, no scratch, no hair
Showed that a cat had once lived there.
He'd wiped the slate completely clean.
It was as if he'd never been.

This brings my story to a close
For where he went to, no-one knows.
My parents let the matter rest
Deciding it was for the best,
Since my distress was plain to see,
To pacify and humour me
And not to try to winkle out
What all the fuss had been about.
Ironically, the only friend
I could confide in in the end
And give a complete catalogue
Of all our doings, was the dog.

As life went on and time went by
We got quite close, that pup and I.
For though he lacked sophistication
(He never grasped the situation)
He was not one to fume and fret
At being someone's special pet.
I'd put him down upon the ground,
He'd sneeze, then start to sniff around
Using his nose with doggy know-how
Just like a little carpet snow-plough.
And then he'd stop and stare and growl
And pounce upon an old tea-towel
And worry it, all teeth and fluff,
To show me he was really tough.

It was the high spot of his day
When I came home from school to play,
I only had to call his name
Wherever he was, he always came
Wagging his tail with sheer delight –
And he did sleep on my bed at night.

Before we slept we'd sit and chat
And wonder all about the cat.
Where was he now? Was he in town?
And would he ever settle down?
Why did he take the hat? To wear,
Or simply as a pied-à-terre?
And since we had no information
We did a lot of speculation,
Picturing him now there, now here,
Embarking on some new career.

I saw him as a great tycoon
Importing catnip from Rangoon,
Or doing deals with catapults
Designed especially for adults.
I saw him too in other guises
Directing major enterprises
From Knightsbridge, Mayfair or the City
Cashing in and sitting pretty.
Perhaps he went to Mrs Thatcher
To be her personal mole-catcher.
Or maybe he got so frustrated
He simply upped and emigrated.
I imagined him in foreign lands
Thinking amid the desert sands,
Or sorting out some frightful bungle

Before we slept we'd sit and chat
And wonder all about the cat

Deep in the Amazonian jungle,
Or charting all the seven seas –
Or once more sitting on my knees.

I must confess I miss him still.
In fact, I think I always will.
And when I hear my puppy snoring
I seem to hear him say 'How boring!'
And see him with his tail held high
Fix us with that great green eye.

He is for ever intertwined
With all these pictures in my mind,
And lives there, with his bowler hat,
My one and only thinking cat.

AUTHOR'S APOLOGY

To the best of my recollection I began this little verse narrative while working for a market research company called MIL in a large office in a building just off Oxford Street in London's West End. The office was a kind of call centre and the main job of the team I was working with, which consisted mainly of young actors waiting for openings, was to ring up people who had just bought new cars or vans and ask them to rate their experience of their vehicle. In the brief gaps between calls, I would jot down couplets, if I could. I continued with this perhaps reprehensible practice when I moved to another company called Quantum and carried on doing much the same work except that the interviews were about other products than cars and were conducted in German and French. So, I owe an apology to MIL and Quantum, if they still exist, for misusing their time.

The Thinking Cat was a green shoot for me towards the end of what were – and will hopefully remain – the worst five years or so of my life. That period, largely coinciding with the recession of the early Thatcher years, ended with the birth of my youngest child, Thomas, in 1983 and my acquisition of a job with a dictionary-publishing company in 1984. Perhaps for this reason I have always had a particularly soft spot for the Thinking Cat. I hope I can persuade contemporary readers to think highly of him too.

THE ILLUSTRATOR

After a career as a television producer with the BBC, Jessica Palmer started an MA in Illustration at the University of Kingston at the age of 49. She is now an independent artist and illustrator. Her work includes paper cutting and paper sculpture in addition to drawing and is featured in illustrations, designs, book covers, commissions and exhibits. She is the author of *The Art of Papercutting, Tangle Wood - A Captivating Colouring Book* and *Tangle Bay: An Enchanting Colouring Book with Hidden Treasure*, all published by Search Press. Jessica is a visiting artist at many galleries including the National Portrait Gallery, the British Museum, the Museum of London, Historic Royal Palaces and the Victoria & Albert Museum, as well as the Holburne Museum in Bath. She is an occasional Bristol Drawing School Tutor where she teaches life drawing and her unique class 'Drawing Life with a Knife'. Jessica is married with two children and lives in Bath. Find out more about her and her work by going to www.jessicapalmerart.com.

THE AUTHOR

Stephen Curtis was born in Hertford, England, and educated at Cheshunt Grammar School, The Queen's College, Oxford, and the University of York.

He has degrees in modern languages and English and has worked as an English lecturer, a milkman, a call-center worker, a translator, a lexicographer, an editor and proofreader, and a writer of innovative English-language teaching books for Singapore and beyond.

Curtis is the author of more than twenty plays and a novel called *A Wonderful Piece of Work* as well as other unpublished stories and poems for children.

55720191R00035

Made in the USA
Charleston, SC
06 May 2016